RAF, DOMINION & ALLIED SQUADRONS AT WAR:
STUDY, HISTORY AND STATISTICS

COMPILED BY
PHIL H. LISTEMANN

Drawings by Claveworks Graphic

PREFACE

The purpose of this study is to provide aviation historians and enthusiasts with a range of information relative to each of the Commonwealth squadrons that saw combat during World War II. Each record will comprise a short history, complete with illustrations and artwork, and accompanied by the following appendices:

Appendix I: Squadron Commanders and Flight Commanders
Appendix II: Major awards
Appendix III: Operational diary (number of sorties per month)
Appendix IV: Victory list
Appendix V: Aircraft losses on operations
Appendix VI: Aircraft losses in accidents
Appendix VII: Aircraft Serial numbers matching with individual letters (including mission totals for multi-engine aircraft)
Appendix VIII: Nominal roll (Captains only for bomber and seaplane units)
Appendix IX: Roll of Honour

Individual files will be constantly updated, when any fresh information comes to light. Additional information will be available for download, at no charge, on each squadron's site at:

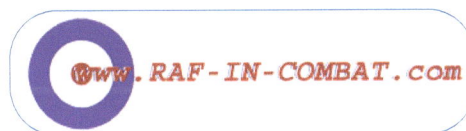

www.RAF-IN-COMBAT.com

GLOSSARY OF TERMS

RANKS

AC: Aircraftman
G/C: Group Captain
W/C: Wing Commander
S/L: Squadron Leader
F/L: Flight Lieutenant
F/O: Flying Officer
P/O: Pilot Officer
W/O: Warrant Officer
F/Sgt: Flight Sergeant
Sgt: Sergeant
Cpl: Corporal
LAC: Leading Aircraftman

OTHER

AAF: Auxiliary Air Force
CO: Commanding Officer
DFC: Distinguished Flying Cross

DFM: Distinguished Flying Medal
DSO: Distinguished Service Order
Eva.: Evaded
Inj.: Injured
ORB: Operational Record Book
OTU: Operational Training Unit
PAF: Polish Air Force
PoW: Prisoner of War
RAF: Royal Air Force
RAAF: Royal Australian Air Force
RCAF: Royal Canadian Air Force
RNZAF: Royal New Zealand Air Force
SAAF: South African Air Force
Sqn: Squadron
TOC: Taken on charge
†: Killed

No.441 (RCAF) Squadron 1944-1945

ISBN: 978-2-918590-61-3

Contributors & Acknowledgments:
Hugh Halliday, Bruce MacKenzie, Larry Milberry
Paul Sortehaug, Andrew Thomas, Chris Thomas

Cover: Spitfire Mk.IXs MA422/9G-Y during an escort flight over Continental Europe in 1945.

Main Equipment

SPITFIRE V	Feb.44 - Mar.44
SPITFIRE IX	Mar.44 - May.45
SPITFIRE V	Jan.45 - Apr.45
MUSTANG III	May.45 - Aug.45

SQUADRON CODE LETTERS:

9G

SQUADRON HISTORY

No.441 (RCAF) Squadron began life as No.125 Squadron, RCAF. It was formed as a fighter unit on 20 April 1942 at Sydney (Nova Scotia), and flew Hurricanes on Canada's East Coast until the end of 1943, when it was selected as one of six home fighter units for European service. During 18 months in Canada personnel had racked up over 500 sorties for the loss of five aircraft and a single pilot, and it was this experience that made the unit a candidate for an overseas assignment.

Arriving in United Kingdom early in 1944, complete in personnel but devoid of aircraft, it was placed under Fighter Command authority and re-designated No.441 Squadron on **8 February 1944**. It received Spitfire Mk.V for equipment to re-train the pilots, who accumulated some 237 hours on type. It was then transferred to No.2 TAF, in preparation for D-Day, and was re-equipped with Spitfire Mk.IXs to continue its training. For the invasion, it became part of No.144 (RCAF) Wing, with two others Canadian squadrons, Nos.442 and 443.

After being reinforced with experienced pilots it was declared operational and the first sorties were performed on 27 March 1944, when F/O William R. Chowen and P/O Leslie C. Saunders scrambled after an unidentified aircraft. The first offensive operation over the Continent was flown the very next day, and the first claim, a probable Me410, was made. With D-Day approaching, the Allied pressure upon Germany increased, as did the number of sorties. During April and May there were a number of claims, but also losses, including the CO on 25 April 1944, who was shot down and taken prisoner. On D-Day some 48 sorties were carried out and on 15 June the squadron began to operate from France. In mid-July, when No.144 Wing was disbanded, No.441 Squadron became part of No.125 Wing and was predominantly employed to cover the Allied troops. At the end of September 1944, after claiming its last victories, three Bf109s on the 27th, the squadron was removed from the 2nd TAF and transferred back to Fighter Command in Britain. At that time it had accumulated 2,800 sorties.

For the next three months, 441 Squadron was flying escort duties for Bomber Command's daylight activities over the Continent. During December, it was stationed in Scotland for a period of rest, which ended in April when it resumed its bomber escort duties from Hawkinge. The last sortie was carried on the 25th, when F/L Alistair Smith led nine Spitfires on an escort (*Ramrod* 1555), without incident. No.441 Squadron participated to the Victory Sweep to Guernsey on 12 May 1945, ending a year of considerable action. During it's European service 21 Spitfires were lost in action, 3 in accidents with 11 pilots killed and 3 reported as being taken prisoner in over 4,600 operational hours and 3,169 sorties. Shortly after VE-Day, the squadron moved to Digby where it converted to the Mustang III. However, following the end of the war in Europe, only 850 flying hours of training was possible before the unit was disbanded on **7 August 1945**.

SQUADRON BASES

Digby	08.02.44 - 18.03.44	Lingrèves/B19 (France)	13.08.44 - 02.09.44
Holmsley South	18.03.44 - 01.04.44	Beauvais-Nivilliers/B40 (France)	02.09.44 - 05.09.44
Westhampnett	01.04.44 - 12.04.44	Douai/B52 (France)	05.09.44 - 17.09.44
Hutton Cranswick	12.04.44 - 23.04.44	Deurne/B70 (Belgium)	17.09.44 - 01.10.44
Funtington	23.04.44 - 13.05.44	Hawkinge	01.10.44 - 30.12.44
Ford	13.05.44 - 15.06.44	Skaebrae	30.12.44 - 03.04.45
Ste-Croix sur Mer/B3 (France)	15.06.44 - 15.07.44	Hawkinge	03.04.45 - 29.04.45
Longues/B11 (France)	15.07.44 - 13.08.44	Hunsdon	29.04.45 - 17.05.45

ARTICLE XV

Shortly after Britain's declaration of war, supported on the same date by Australia and New Zealand, and Canada a week later, the British Government asked Commonwealth countries to supply partially trained aircrew for the expansion of the RAF. In those years prior to the war an allocation of men from the Dominions had been offered Short Service, or Permanent, Commission in the RAF, but the speed with which the Nazis had overrun Poland, made it clear that large numbers of airmen would be needed urgently. In November 1939, the Ottawa (Canada) Conference formulated the setting-up of the Empire Air Training Scheme (EATS) to train aircrew to a uniform standard in each of the Dominions previously mentioned, and subsequently South Africa, which was already operating a scheme, and Rhodesia.

Desirous of exercising some control over its own nationals, which was not the case for those who had joined up prior to the war, Canada obtained, via Article XV, an agreement that their aircrew would be gathered together in national squadrons, to serve alongside the permanent units of the RAF. For operational and administrative reasons Australia and New Zealand were reluctant to establish and maintain RAAF or RNZAF squadrons in Britain so eventually it was decided that units formed in the RAF would be identified with them.

In order to distinguish those units created under Article XV the RAF reserved a block of numbers commencing with 400 which was allocated to them. The RCAF squadrons were to start with 400, the RAAF, 450 and the RNZAF, 485. From the start aircrew were paid at the rates of pay in force in their respective countries, and depended on the RAF for aircraft and logistical support.

Their operational deployment was to be determined by the RAF, even though respective Governments of each of the Dominions retained an overview on their airmen. Some existing squadrons were re-numbered in the new series to avoid confusion with established RAF units. As an example No.1 Squadron RCAF, which was sent to support Great Britain in 1940, was subsequently re-numbered No.401 (RCAF) Squadron. The policy behind Article XV Squadrons provided a greater national identity to those countries who were able to identify themselves in their title e.g. No.441 (RCAF) Squadron.

Initially the RAF supplied the vast majority of the ground personnel for most of the Commonwealth squadrons. The aircrew posted to these squadrons represented only some, and not all, of that particular country's nationals. Indeed almost every squadron in the RAF at some time or another had members amongst their ranks from all of the Dominions- aircrew were sent where there was the greatest need for them.

In the beginning the authorities attempted to relocate serving RAF officers to those newly formed squadrons from their Dominions. However this was not always possible or practical, especially where senior positions needed to be filled. As a result British or other nationals frequently filled the vacancies in these squadrons. Regrettably friction between nationalities sometimes occurred, although this was not a major problem. The posting or replacement of certain personnel would generally defuse such situations.

By the end of the war Article XV Squadrons had proved that they were equal to the best that the RAF had produced and had no need to be envious of their British counterparts. Not only had they achieved impressive operational records but they gave the Dominions a renewed confidence and pride in their military ability.

Of the Dominions Canada became the biggest contributor, providing 44 operational squadrons between 1941 and 1944. Eight of these were sourced from Home RCAF squadrons, and, of the 44 squadrons, thirteen were of the day-fighter type.

APPENDIX I
SQUADRON AND FLIGHT COMMANDERS

Rank and Name	SN	Origin	Dates
W/C James E. **WALKER** [1]	CAN./J.3199	RCAF	08.02.44 - 11.03.44
S/L George U. **HILL** *(PoW)*	CAN./C.1075	RCAF	11.03.44 - 25.04.44
S/L John D. **BROWNE**	CAN./J.9068	(US)/RCAF	26.04.44 - 01.07.44
S/L Thomas A. **BRANNAGAN** *(PoW)*	CAN./J.10762	RCAF	01.07.44 - 15.08.44
S/L Roy H. **WALKER**	CAN./J.9425	RCAF	26.08.44 - 07.08.45

[1] : Between 08.02.44 and 11.03.44 the Squadron was commanded by No.144 Airfield CO.

A FLIGHT

Rank and Name	SN	Origin	Dates
F/L Guy E. **MOTT**	CAN./J.22319	RCAF	08.02.44 - 11.03.44
F/L Leslie A. **MOORE**	CAN./J.17857	RCAF	11.03.44 - 22.07.44
F/L Guy E. **MOTT**	CAN./J.22319	RCAF	22.07.44 - 12.12.44
F/L Donald H. **KIMBALL**	CAN./J.35983	RCAF	12.12.44 - 07.08.45

B FLIGHT

Rank and Name	SN	Origin	Dates
F/L John W. **GILMARTIN**	CAN./J.22318	RCAF	08.02.44 - 11.03.44
F/L Thomas A. **BRANNAGAN**	CAN./J.10762	RCAF	11.03.44 - 01.07.44
F/L William W.L. **BROWN** *(†)*	CAN./J.16571	RCAF	01.07.44 - 13.08.44
F/L Alistair A. **SMITH**	CAN./J.6496	RCAF	14.08.44 - 07.08.45

APPENDIX II
MAJOR AWARDS

DSO: -

DFC: 8
Thomas Anthony **BRANNAGAN** (CAN./J.10762 - RCAF)
Donald Harold **KIMBALL** (CAN./J.35983 - RCAF)
Ronald George **LAKE** (CAN./J.11283 - RCAF)
Leslie Albert **MOORE** (CAN./J.17857 - RCAF)
Guy Elwood **MOTT** (CAN./J.22319 - RCAF)
William James **MYERS** (CAN./J.18688 - RCAF)
Alistair Angus **SMITH** (CAN./J.6496 - RCAF)
Frederick Albert William Johnson **WILSON** (CAN./J.85876 - RCAF)

DFM: -

APPENDIX III
Operational Diary
Number of Sorties per Month

Date	Month	Total		Date	Month	Total
Mar.44	25	25		Jan.45	4	3,085
Apr.44	117	142		Feb.45	-	3,085
May.44	323	465		Mar.45	-	3,085
Jun.44	550	1,015		Apr.45	74	3,159
Jul.44	713	1,728		May.45	10	3,169
Aug.44	619	2,347				
Sep.44	411	2,758		**Grand Total**		**3,169**
Oct.44	121	2,879				
Nov.44	112	2,991		Extracted from AIR27/1881		
Dec.44	90	3,081				

APPENDIX IV
Victory list
Confirmed (C) and Probable (P) claims

Date	Pilot	SN	Origin	Type	Serial	Code	Nb	Cat.

Spitfire IX

Date	Pilot	SN	Origin	Type	Serial	Code	Nb	Cat.
28.03.44	F/O Ronald G. Lake	Can./J.11283	RCAF	Me410	MK504	9G-L	0.5	P
	F/L Guy E. Mott	Can./J.22319	RCAF		MK177	9G-A	0.5	P
25.04.44	S/L George U. Hill	Can./C.1075	RCAF	Fw190	MK519		0.5	C
	P/O Richard H. Sparling	Can./J.29535	RCAF		MK594		0.5	C
	F/O James W. Fleming	Can./J.25138	RCAF	Fw190	MK315	2I-C*	0.5	C
	F/O Lloyd A. Plummer	Can./J.26508	RCAF		MK632		0.5	C
28.04.44	F/L Thomas A. Brannagan	Can./J.10762	RCAF	Caudron	MK515	9G-W	0.5	C
	F/L Leslie A. Moore	Can./J.17857	RCAF		MK415		0.5	C
05.05.44	P/O Frederick A.W.J. Wilson	Can./J.85676	RCAF	Fw190	MK399	9G-K	1.0	C
	P/O Thomas C. Gamey	Can./J.28753	RCAF	Fw190	MK630	9G-R	1.0	C
22.06.44	F/O James W. Fleming	Can./J.25138	RCAF	Fw190	MK632		1.0	C
	F/O William W.L. Brown	Can./J.16571	RCAF	Fw190	MK992	9G-J	0.33	C
	F/O William R. Chowen	Can./J.26678	RCAF		NH306		0.33	C
	F/Sgt Ross A. McMillan	Can./R.156192	RCAF		MK630	9G-R	0.33	C
30.06.44	S/L John D. Browne	Can./J.9068	(US)/RCAF	Fw190	ML205	9G-C	1.0	C
	F/L Alan Johnstone	Can./J.5210	(US)/RCAF	Bf109	ML269	9G-B	1.0	C
	F/L Guy E. Mott	Can./J.22319	RCAF	Bf109	PL274	9G-K	1.0	C
02.07.44	F/O Alexander J. McDonald	Can./J.26034	RCAF	Fw190	ML213		1.0	C
	F/L Leslie A. Moore	Can./J.17857	RCAF	Bf109	ML269	9G-B	2.5	C
	F/O Ronald G. Lake	Can./J.11283	RCAF		MK504	9G-L	1.5	C
				Fw190	MK504	9G-L	1.0	C
05.07.44	F/O Donald H. Kimball	Can./J.35983	RCAF	Fw190	MK239	9G-D	1.0	C

	S/L Thomas A. **Brannagan**	Can./J.10762	RCAF	Fw190	**MK907**			1.0	C
	F/O John W. **Neil**	Can./J.16638	RCAF	Fw190	**NH306**			1.0	C
	F/O William R. **Chowen**	Can./J.26678	RCAF	Fw190	**MH756**			1.5	C
	F/L Guy E. **Mott**	Can./J.22319	RCAF		**PL274**	9G-K		1.5	C
13.07.44	S/L Thomas A. **Brannagan**	Can./J.10762	RCAF	Fw190	**NH320**	9G-W		2.0	C
	F/O William J. **Myers**	Can./18688	RCAF	Fw190	**ML205**	9G-C		3.0	C
	F/L Guy E. **Mott**	Can./J.22319	RCAF	Fw190	**PL274**	9G-K		1.0	C
	F/O Donald H. **Kimball**	Can./J.35983	RCAF	Fw190	**MJ477**	9G-Q		1.0	C
	F/L Jack C. **Copeland**	Can./J.9421	RCAF	Fw190	**MK415**			1.0	C
	F/O Bruce M. **MacKenzie**	Can./J.23797	RCAF	Fw190	**MK417**	9G-M		1.0	C
	F/O Lloyd A. **Plummer**	Can./J.26508	RCAF	Fw190	**MK852**			1.0	C
17.07.44	F/L William W.L. **Brown**	Can./J.16571	RCAF	Fw190	**NH398**	9G-O		2.0	C
	F/O Donald H. **Kimball**	Can./J.35983	RCAF	Fw190	**MJ477**	9G-Q		1.0	C
18.07.44	F/L Guy E. **Mott**	Can./J.22319	RCAF	Bf109	**MK135**			1.0	C
	F/L Jack C. **Copeland**	Can./J.9421	RCAF	Bf109	**MK415**			0.5	C
	F/L Alan **Johnstone**	Can./J.5210	(us)/RCAF		**ML268**			0.5	C
27.07.44	F/O Donald H. **Kimball**	Can./J.35983	RCAF	Fw190	**MJ477**	9G-Q		1.0	C
	F/L Guy E. **Mott**	Can./J.22319	RCAF	Fw190	**MK504**	9G-L		1.0	C
18.09.44	S/L Roy H. **Walker**	Can./J.9425	RCAF	Bf109	**ML370**	9G-K		0.5	C
	F/L Alan **Johnstone**	Can./J.5210	(us)/RCAF		**ML360**			0.5	C
	F/O George E. **Heasman**	Can./J.36362	RCAF	Bf109	**ML271**			1.0	C
	F/L Ronald G. **Lake**	Can./J.11283	RCAF	Bf109	**ML317**	9G-L		1.0	C
25.09.44	F/O Harrold E. **Derraugh**	Can./J.26045	RCAF	Bf109	**MK967**	9G-E		1.0	C
	F/O Donald H. **Kimball**	Can./J.35983	RCAF	Bf109	**ML141**	9G-H		2.0	C
27.09.44	P/O Sid **Bregman**	Can./J.23894	RCAF	Bf109	**MJ627**	9G-Q		1.0	C
	F/L Jack C. **Copeland**	Can./J.9421	RCAF	Bf109	**PL272**	9G-A		1.0	C
	F/L Ronald G. **Lake**	Can./J.11283	RCAF	Bf109	**MK267**			1.0	C

*Aircraft on loan from No.443 (RCAF) Sqn.

Total: 49.0

Aircraft damaged: 9.0

APPENDIX V
AIRCRAFT LOST ON OPERATIONS

Date	Pilot		S/N	Origin	Serial	Code	Mark	Fate

SPITFIRE

25.04.44 S/L George U. **Hill**   Can/C.1075   RCAF   **MK519**   LF.IXB   **PoW**

Took off at 07.20 with 11 others for RAMROD 783, leading the formation. Intercepted six Fw190s of 12./JG2 over the Laon area and was shot down; crashed near Laon (France). Became a PoW at Stalag Luft 1. RCAF regular officer, he previously served in Europe with Nos.453 (RAAF) and 403 (RCAF) Sqns and then the Med with No.111 Sqn taking command of the unit at the end of his tour (April - August 1943). 18 confirmed victories, 8 being shared, DFC & 2 Bars [all with No.111 Sqn].
Note on the aircraft: TOC No.8 MU 28.02.44, issued No.441 Sqn 13.03.44.

P/O Richard H. **Sparling**   Can./J.29535   RCAF   **MK394**   LF.IXB   †

Took off at 07.20 with 11 others for Ramrod 783, the CO leading. As above. Canadian form Ontario, he was an original member of the squadron, and formerly with No.125 Sqn, RCAF.
Note on the aircraft: TOC No.8 MU 20.02.44, issued No.441 Sqn 13.03.44.

05.05.44   F/O Percy A. **McLachlan**   Can./J.16591   RCAF   **MJ473**   LF.IXB   †

Took off at 06.55 with 11 others for RAMROD 831, the CO leading. Engaged and shot down by FW190s of III./JG26 and crashed

near Mons (Belgium). Had been a member of the squadron since March and had previously served with No.421 (RCAF) Sqn. Canadian from British Columbia, he was serving overseas since February 1942.
<u>Note on the aircraft</u>: TOC No.33 MU 15.11.43, issued No.441 Sqn 23.03.44.

05.06.44   F/Sgt Victorin A.G. **Brochu**   Can./R.55845   RCAF   **MK465**   9G-F   LF.IXB   -
Took off with 11 others for a shipping patrol at 22.10, the CO leading the formation. Engine failure in flight and forced to bale out over the Channel. Pilot picked up 42 hours later off the coast of France. An original member of the squadron, and formerly with No.125 Sqn, RCAF. Later killed with the squadron (see entry 28.10.44).
<u>Note on the aircraft</u>: TOC No.8 MU 02.02.44, issued No.441 Sqn 13.03.44.

08.06.44   F/L Alan **Johnstone**   Can./J.5210   (us)/RCAF   **MK460**   LF.IXB   -
Took off at 15.35 with 11 others p²roviding low cover for the Assault area (beachhead). Engine failed on take-off and belly-landed five minutes later in a field near Hansham, Sussex. Pilot unhurt. F/L Johnstone served in Canada with Nos.118 and 132 Sqns, RCAF, in 1942 -1943 before being sent to the UK in August 1943 and posted to the Squadron in April 1944 as supernumerary Flight Lieutenant. He left prematurely on 02.11.44, when he became victim of a flying accident whilst flying Spitfire EP388, a Hawkinge Station Flight aircraft. He returned to the squadron on 30.04.45 but was sent to 'R' depot for repatriation four days later. An American pilot who enlisted in September 1940.
<u>Note on the aircraft</u>: TOC No.8 MU 20.01.44, issued No.441 Sqn 24.03.44.

12.06.44   F/O Charles A. **Graham**   Can./J.15544   RCAF   **MK466**   9G-G   LF.IXB   **Inj.**
Took off with with 11 others providing low cover of the Assault area (beachhead) at 11.25. One tyre burst on take-off causing the aircraft to nose over and seriously injure the pilot. Graham had joined the squadron in March and had previously served with Nos.91, 411 (RCAF) and 402 (RCAF) Sqns. Canadian from Regina, Saskachewan.
<u>Note on the aircraft</u>: TOC No.8 MU 20.02.44, issued No.441 Sqn 13.03.44.

        P/O John E. **West**   Can./J.35957   RCAF   **MH447**   LF.IXB   †
Took off with 11 others for a low cover of the Assault area in Normandy at 15.40 the CO leading the formation. Engine failure on the return flight and forced to bale out over the Channel. The parachute caught on the tail of the aircraft, carrying him under the water. An original member of the squadron, and formerly with Nos. 126 & 125 Sqns, RCAF. Canadian from Nova Scotia.
<u>Note on the aircraft</u>: TOC No.129 Sqn 12.08.43, issued No.441 Sqn 20.05.44. Previously served with No.504 Sqn.

15.06.44   P/O Arthur J. **Horrell**   Can./J.21413   RCAF   **MK399**   9G-K   LF.IXB   -
Took off at 22.55 with eleven others on scramble. Engine failure and attempted to land to St-Croix sur mer (France), but over shot the runway due to brake failure. Pilot had just arrived from No.443 (RCAF) Sqn that morning and was posted back two days later. Killed four months later on 11.10.44 while flying Auster NJ669.
<u>Note on the aircraft</u>: TOC No.8 MU 12.02.44, issued No.441 Sqn 13.03.44.

30.06.44   F/O John W. **Fleming**   Can./J.25138   RCAF   **MK737**   9G-K   LF.IXB   **PoW**
Took off with 10 others at 12.15 for an armed reconnaissance over Harcourt-Flers-Condé-Falaise area. Shot down by Fw190s near Gace, becoming a PoW in Stalag Luft 1. An original member of the squadron, and formerly with No.125 Sqn, RCAF.
<u>Note on the aircraft</u>: TOC No.39 MU 12.03.44, issued No.441 Sqn date unrecorded, from No.132 Sqn which took of charge the aircraft on 15.06.44 but that seems to be a mistake as MK737 is tracable as early as 19.05.44 in No.441 Sqn's records.

02.07.44   P/O Alexander J. **McDonald**   Can./J.26034   RCAF   **ML213**   LF.IXB   **Eva.**
Took off at 12.00 with 11 others for a patrol over the front line, the CO leading the formation. Intercepted 8-10 German fighters 3 m west of Lisieux. Shot down by Bf109s, captured but later evaded. Returned to the unit on 17.08.44. Founder member of the squadron, formerly with No.125 Sqn, RCAF. Later killed with the squadron (see entry 28.10.44).
<u>Note on the aircraft</u>: TOC No.8 MU 27.04.44, issued No.441 Sqn 15.05.44.

05.07.44 F/O William R. **Chowen** Can./J.26678 RCAF **MH756** LF.IXB †
Took off with 10 others for an armed reconnaissance of Evreux-Chartres area at 18.15, the CO leading. Intercepted 13 Fw190s over Alençon and was shot down. Canadian from Ontario, he was an original member of the squadron, and formerly with No.125 Sqn, RCAF.
Note on the aircraft: TOC No.33 MU 19.09.43, issued No.441 Sqn date unrecorded. Previously served with No.317 (Polish) Sqn. While serving with No.441 Sqn, MH756 was usually flown by F/O L.A. Plummer since it appeared in squadron's records on 28.06.44.

06.08.44 F/L Guy E. **Mott** Can./J.22319 RCAF **MJ419** LF.IXB **Eva.**
Took off with 3 others for an armed reconnaissance south of the front line at 17.00. Hit by flak and baled out near Condé, returning to the squadron three days later. An original member of the squadron, and formerly with No.125 Sqn, RCAF and had served previously with No.14 Sqn, RCAF in Canada. he left the squadron in December 1944.
Note on the aircraft: TOC No.9 MU 05.11.43, issued No.441 Sqn date not recorded. F/L Mott used to fly this aircraft since it appeared in the 441 Sqn's records on 29.07.44.

13.08.44 F/L William W.L. **Brown** Can./J.16571 RCAF **NH178** 9G-O LF.IXB †
Took off with 11 others for an armed reconnaissance NW of Flers at 18.00. Hit by flak attacking MET and turned for base. He was seen by his No.2 (F/O L.G. Saunders) to go into a spin about 10 m east of Vire. Brown, a Canadian from Alberta, had joined the squadron in May and was serving overseas since August 1941.
Note on the aircraft: TOC No.46 MU 30.04.44, issued No.441 Sqn 10.08.44.

15.08.44 S/L Thomas A. **Brannagan** Can./J.10562 RCAF **NH233** 9G-H LF.IXB **PoW**
Took off at 17.30 with 11 others for an armed reconnaissance over Bernay area. Shot down by flighters, becoming a PoW in Stalag Luft III. Previously served with No.403 (RCAF) Sqn.
Note on the aircraft: TOC No.45 MU 08.05.44, issued No.441 Sqn date unrecorded, but No.441 Sqn's ORB, it appears that it was its first operational flight.

14.09.44 F/L Raymond G. **Sim** Can./J.6947 RCAF **NH405** LF.IXB **Eva.**
Took off at 13.10 with 3 others for an armed reconnaissance over Flushing area (Holland). Hit by flak attacking MET and baled out. He was seen to land safely and enter a nearby farmhouse where he was met by two Dutch civilians. Arrived back in the UK at the end of October. Sim had originally joined the squadron in July. Later posted to No.443 (RCAF) Sqn.
Note on the aircraft: TOC No.9 MU 24.04.44, issued No.441 Sqn 17.08.44.

25.09.44 F/L Bernard **Boe** Can./J.3463 RCAF **ML360** LF.IXB †
Took off at 14.35 with 10 others for a patrol over Nijmegen area (Holland). Encountered 30 Bf109s and Fw190s about to attack the bridgehead there. Shot down during the ensuing dogfight. 'Barney' Boe from British Columbia had joined the squadron in August.
Note on the aircraft: TOC No.9 MU 21.04.44, issued No.441 Sqn 17.08.44.

F/Sgt Osman **McMillan** Can./R.154163 RCAF **NH151** 9G-S LF.IXB †
Took off at 14.35 with 10 others for a patrol over Nijmegen area (Holland). As above. An original member of the squadron, and formerly with No.125 Sqn, RCAF he was coming from Ontario.
Note on the aircraft: TOC No.8 MU 30.04.44, issued No.441 Sqn 17.08.44.

26.09.44 F/O James A. **McIntosh** Can./J.27247 RCAF **NH176** 9G-Y LF.IXB -
Took off at 16.00 with 10 other for a patrol over Nijmegen area. Hit by Bf109s and forced landed at B.78. McIntosh had joined the squadron in August. McIntosh served the squadron until disdandment in August 1945.
Note on the aircraft: TOC No.46 MU 30.04.44, issued No.441 Sqn 24.08.44.

28.10.44 F/O Alexander J. **McDonald** Can./J.26034 RCAF **MK602** LF.IXB †
Took of at 14.55 with 13 others as escort for Lancasters targeting Cologne (Germany). Last seen about to descend through

clouds south of Brussels (Belgium) on the return journey. Presumed his aircraft had iced-up. 'Alex' McDonald, a Canadian from Ontario, was an original member of the squadron, and formerly with No.125 Sqn, RCAF.

Note on the aircraft: TOC No.9 MU 02.01.44, issued No.441 Sqn 06.09.44.Served also with No.443 (RCAF) Sqn.

| | P/O Victorin A.G. **Brochu** | Can./J.88814 | RCAF | **MJ301** | | LF.IXB | † |

Took of at 14.55 with 13 others as escort for Lancasters targeting Cologne (Germany). Last seen about to descend through clouds south of Brussels (Belgium) on the return journey. Presumed his aircraft had iced-up. (See also entry 05.06.44). 'Gil' Brochu from the province of Quebec was serving the Squadron since July.

Note on the aircraft: TOC No.9 MU 08.11.43, issued No.441 Sqn 10.09.44.

| 16.11.44 | F/O Arthur B. **Jewett** | Can./J.35218 | RCAF | **MJ453** | | LF.IXB | - |

Took off at 14.15 with 12 others for RAMROD 1372 (Duren). Engine failure over the target but was able to abandon the aircraft over the Allied lines. Jewett had joined the squadron in July and left in August 45.

Note on the aircraft: TOC No.9 MU 29.11.43, issued No.441 Sqn 28.09.44.

Total: 21

```
┌─────────────────────────────┐
│        APPENDIX VI          │
│  AIRCRAFT LOST IN ACCIDENTS │
└─────────────────────────────┘
```

SPITFIRE

| 18.11.44 | - | | - | - | **ML317** | 9G-L | LF.IXB | - |

Caught fire during start up procedure by ground crew.

Note on the aircraft: TOC No.33 MU 13.05.44, issued No.441 Sqn 17.08.44.

| 08.01.45 | F/O Harrold E. **Derraugh** | Can./J.26045 | RCAF | **EE722** | | VC | - |

After having been ferried from MU, the aircraft was blown over while taxying on the runway due to a combination of a strong wind gust and incorrect operation of brakes. Pilot escaped without injuries. EE722, was one of a few Spitfire Mk.Vs used for training while the squadron was stationed at Skebrae. Harold Derraugh had joined the Squadron in August 44 and left one year later.

Note on the aircraft: TOC No.39 MU 09.11.42, issued No.441 Sqn at a unrcorded date but was on 441 Sqn charge when the aircraft was wrecked. Served also with Nos.234 and 130 Sqns.

| 23.01.45 | W/O1 Joseph E. **Bohemier** | Can./R.101950 | RCAF | **MK585** | 9G-S | LF.IXB | † |

Missing from exercise off the Shetland Islands. Canadian from the province of Quebec, he was an original member of the squadron, and formerly with No.125 Sqn, RCAF.

Note on the aircraft: TOC No.8 MU 26.03.44, issued No.441 Sqn 28.09.44. Served also with No.56 Sqn.

| 10.03.45 | F/L Ernest W. **Martin** | Can./J.12780 | RCAF | **ML216** | | HF.IXB | † |

Took off at 11.35 with F/O R.W. Perkin for a GCI excercice. Pilots were soon separated and control lost contact with F/L Martin who was posted missing. Was serving the squadron since December 1944. Canadian from Ontario, he served as flying instructor in Canada for two years before to be posted overseas mid-1944.

Note on the aircraft: TOC No.39 MU 13.04.44, issued No.441 Sqn 15.02.44. Previously served with Nos.127, 313 (Czech) & 118 Sqns.

24.07.45   F/O Edward J. McCabe   Can./J.43958   RCAF   **KH569**   III   †
Lost control while flying in turbulent cloud conditions during a cross country flight. Crashed Clough Road Hull. McCabe had only joined the squadron earlier that month and was serving overseas since January 1945 . Canadian from Ontario.
Note on the aircraft: Built as P-51C-10-NT 44-10994. Sailed to the UK 24.08.44, No.20 MU 14.11.44. Issued No.441 Sqn 31.05.45. Served previously with Nos.118 and 165 Sqns.

APPENDIX VII
Aircraft serial numbers matching with individual letters

9G-A
MJ344, NH418, PL272 (*Spitfire IX*)
9G-B
ML269 (*Spitfire IX*)
9G-C
ML205 (*Spitfire IX*)
KH580 (*Mustang III*)
9G-D
MK239 (*Spitfire IX*)
9G-E
MA528, MJ528, MK375, MK967
(*Spitfire IX*)
FZ190 (*Mustang III*)
9G-F
MK465, NH313 (*Spitfire IX*)
9G-G
MK466 (*Spitfire IX*)
9G-H
MH420, ML141 (*Spitfire IX*)
9G-I

9G-J
MJ504, MK992 (*Spitfire IX*)
9G-K
MK399, ML370, NH209, PL274
(*Spitfire IX*)
9G-L
MK504, ML317 (*Spitfire IX*)
HB876 (*Mustang III*)
9G-M
MH257, MJ420, MK257, MK417
(*Spitfire IX*)
HB859 (*Mustang III*)
9G-N
MA420 (*Spitfire IX*)
9G-O
NH998, NH178 (*Spitfire IX*)
9G-P
NH306 (*Spitfire IX*)
9G-Q
MA528, MJ627, MK737 (*Spitfire IX*)
9G-R

MH630, MK926 (*Spitfire IX*)
9G-S
MK201, MK585, ML251 (*Spitfire IX*)
KH495 (*Mustang III*)
9G-T
MJ584 (*Spitfire IX*)
9G-U

9G-V

9G-W
MK341, MK515, ML345, NH320
(*Spitfire IX*)
9G-X
MJ139, MK213 (*Spitfire IX*)
9G-Y
MA422, ML196, NH176 (*Spitfire IX*)
KH466 (*Mustang III*)
9G-Z
EN555 (*Spitfire IX*)

APPENDIX VIII
LIST OF KNOWN PILOTS POSTED OR ATTACHED TO THE SQUADRON

RCAF

C.F. Armstrong, Can./J.22049
W.J. Bentley, Can./J.18929
P.G. Blades, Can./J.6371
B. Boe, Can./J.3463
J.E. Bohemier, Can./J.93491
J.A. Brannagan, Can./J.10762
S. Bregman, Can./J.23894
V.A.G. Brochu, Can./J.88814
W.W.L. Brown, Can./J.16571
J.D. Browne, Can./J.9068, *USA*
D. Brunton, Can./J.35958
T.S. Burleigh, Can./J.16452
T.L. Cashman, Can./J.26684
W.R. Chowen, Can./J.26678

J.C. Copeland, Can./J.9421
J.W. Cronk, Can./J.13469
H.E. Derraugh, Can./J.26045
F.H. Dewar, Can./J.28102
G.C. Draper, Can./J.9439
B.W Dunning, Can./J.19678
C.J. Ernewein, Can./J.91056
J.W. Fleming, Can./J.25138
T.C. Gamey, Can./J.28753
D.C. Gildner, Can./ J.41280
J.W. Gilmartin, Can./J.22318
C.A. Graham, Can./J.15544
R.T. Greer, Can./J.86792
D.A. Hall, Can./J.12288
R.N. Harrison, Can./J.13087
I.J. Hart, Can./J.94446

G.E. Heasman, Can./J.36362
G.U. Hill, Can./C.1075
W.D. Hill, Can./J.35989
A.J. Horrell, Can./J.21413
A.B. Jewett, Can./J.35218
A. Johnstone, Can./J.5210, *USA*
D.H. Kimball, Can./J.35983
R.J. Lacerte, Can./J.28908
R.G. Lake, Can./J.11283
W.U. Lethbridge, Can./J.18561
B.M. MacKenzie, Can./J.23797
E.W. Martin, Can./J.12780
E.J. McCabe, Can./J.43858
J.J. McCann, Can./J.26040
E.G. McClinton, Can./J.93752
A.J. McDonald, Can./J.26034

J.A. **McIntosh**, Can./J.27247
P.A. **McLachlan**, Can./J.16591
O. **McMillan**, Can./J.92574
R.A. **McMillan**, Can./R.156192
D.A. **Mitchell**, Can./J.29891
F.H. **Monette**, Can./J.14872
L.A. **Moore**, Can./J.17857
G.D. **Morrisson**, Can./J.28374
G.E. **Mott**, Can./J.22319
W.J. **Myers**, Can./J.18688
J.W. **Neil**, Can./J.16638
H.K. **O'Brien**, Can./J.18368
R.L. **Paterson**, Can./J.6810
H.R. **Plewes**, Can./J.36706
L.A. **Plummer**, Can./J.26508
E.L. **Prizer**, Can./J.20224
R.W. **Perkin**, Can./J.38572

H.M. **Ritchie**, Can./J.18712
R.H. **Sabel**, Can./J.94116
L.C. **Saunders**, Can./J.39816
R.G. **Sim**, Can./J.6947
A.A. **Smith**, Can./J.6496
R.H. **Sparling**, Can./J.29535
R.H. **Walker**, Can./J.9425
J.E. **West**, Can./J.35957
F.A.W.J. **Wilson**, Can./J.85676
J.T. **Wilson**, Can./J.21018
W. **Wright**, Can./C.94647

APPENDIX IX
ROLL OF HONOUR
†

AIRCREW

Name	Service No	Rank	Age	Origin	Date	Serial
BOE, Bernard	Can./J.3463	F/L	28	RCAF	25.09.44	MJ543
BOHEMEIR, Joseph Eloi	Can./J.93491	P/O	27	RCAF	23.01.45	MK585
BROCHU, Victorin Armand Gilbert	Can./J.88814	P/O	22	RCAF	28.10.44	MJ301
BROWN, William Wood Lindsay	Can./J.16571	F/L	27	RCAF	13.08.44	NH178
CHOWEN, William Ronald	Can./J.26678	F/O	24	RCAF	05.07.44	MH756
MARTIN, Ernest William	Can./J.12780	F/L	24	RCAF	10.03.45	ML216
McCABE, Edward William	Can./J.43958	F/O	21	RCAF	24.07.45	KH569
McDONALD, Alexander James	Can./J.26034	F/O	23	RCAF	28.10.44	MK602
McLACHLAN, Percy Alan	Can./J.16591	F/O	23	RCAF	05.05.44	MJ473
McMILLAN, Osman	Can./J.92574	P/O	21	RCAF	25.09.44	NH151
SPARLING, Richard Herbert	Can./J.29535	P/O	20	RCAF	25.04.44	MK394
WEST, John Edward	Can./J.35957	P/O	26	RCAF	12.06.44	MH447

Total: 12

Canada: 12

GROUNDCREW
Nil

With the Hawker Typhoon, the Supermarine Spitfire Mk.IX was the mainstay of fighter-bomber squadrons of the 2 Tactical Air Force and ADGB in 1944 and 1945. No.441 Squadron Spitfires are seen during various stages of use. 9G-H/ML141 was photographed during either August or September 1944 and was usually flown by Pilot Officer Hugh Ritchie or Flying Officer Leo Cashman. In the background, 9G-A (probably PL272) awaits its pilot, normally Flying Officer H.R Plewes. The two other Spitfires with D-Day markings (below) were usually Pilot Officer Sid Bregman (9G-Q/MJ627) and Flight Lieutenant Guy Mott (9G-K/NH209) machines.

Below left: Spitfire 9G-Q/MA528, usually flown by the CO, Squadron Leader 'Kelly' Walker during 1945, after the squadron had been transferred back to the UK under ADGB. (*All via Larry Milberry*)

Spitfire Mk.IXs during an escort flight over Continental Europe in 1945. Note the new upper wing roundels introduced in January 1945. Sid Bregman is flying 9G-Y/MA422. (via Larry Millberry).

No.441 Sqn converted to Mustang IIIs too late for operational usage. Most were camouflaged in the manner of 9G-Y, but a handful were left in natural metal finish - NMF like 9G-L.
(*via Andrew Thomas*).

Pilots of No.441 Sqn at Funtington in May 1944.
Standing left to right: Jake Fleming (PoW 30.06.44), Alex McDonald (†28.10.44), Bill Dunning, Don Kimball, Alex Graham (Inj.12.06.44), Tom Gamey, Leo Cashman, Wally Hill, Freddie Wilson, Sandy Saunders, Lou Plummer, Bruce MacKenzie and Alan Johnstone (Inj.02.11.44).
In front: Johnnie West (†12.06.44), Guy Mott, Tom Brannagan (PoW 15.08.44), Danny Browne, Les Moore and Bill Draper. (*via Larry Milberry*)

Below left, Thomas Brannagan who was Scottish-born. He was educated in Canada and enlisted in the Windsor Scottish Regiment prior to joining the RCAF in July 1941. He served with No.403 (RCAF) Sqn for a year, claiming a shared victory, before being posted to No.441 Sqn in March 1944 and taking charge of B Flight. Elevated to command the squadron in July, he was shot down and made a PoW on 15 August 1944. His tally amounted to five enemy aircraft destroyed, two being shared.
Below right, Don Kimball was a Canadian from New Brunswick who enlisted in April 1941. He was one of the original pilots drawn from No.125 Sqn, RCAF, in Canada. By the end of the war, he was leading A Flight, and had claimed six aircraft destroyed.

Soon after the beginning of the operational activity, No.441 Sqn lost a couple of experienced pilots in April 1944. Among them, the CO, George U. Hill who had joined the Squadron in March. Native of Nova Scotia, Canada, he was serving overseas since 1942 and distinguished himself while serving with No.111 Sqn in Mediterranean with which he claimed most of his 18 confirmed victories and its awards (DFC and 2 Bars). Shot down by Fw190s, he spent the rest of the war as a PoW. At the conclusion of hostilities, he left the RCAF and became a doctor. *(Author's collection)*

Below: 'Kelly' Walker became the last and the longest-serving CO, being in charge from August 1944 to August 1945, when the squadron disbanded. His previous service was with another Canadian squadron, No.416, with whom he claimed a confirmed victory. *(via Larry Milberry)*

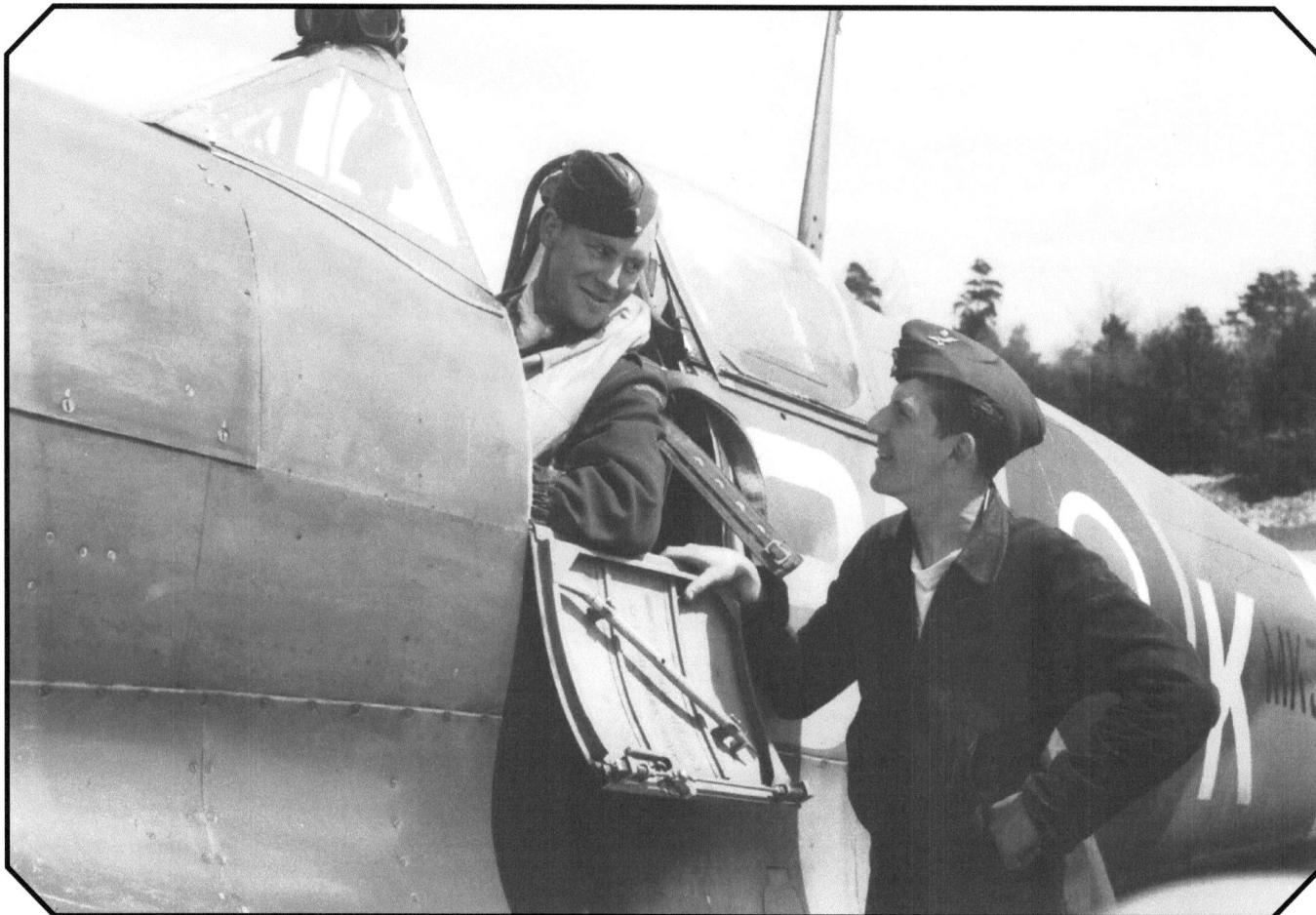

Above, two pilots who by coincidence served with the 441 while they met each other when they were young students in Toronto. In the aircraft MK399/9G-K, 'Jake' Fleming, and 'Lou Plummer standing aside. 'Jake' Fleming became also a PoW while serving the 441. (*Author's collection*)
Below, Charles A. 'Alex' Graham with his Spitfire 'Pam', after the first name of a woman he later married with. Native of Regina, Graham joined the RCAF in 1941 and was posted overseas. He started his operational career with No.91 Sqn, then joined No.411 (RCAF) Sqn in October 1942 and No.402 (RCAF) Sqn in March 1943. In March 1944 he joined in as being some of the few experienced pilots posted in. He was severely injured in June 1944 making an end to his flying career. (*Author's collection*)

Above, typical Normandy informal photo showing from left to right, 'Lou' Plummer, 'Tom' Brannagan and 'Bill' Myers. (*via Larry Milberry*)
Below left: Many Americans continued to serve either the RAF either the RCAF after the USA entered into War. Alan Johnstone is one of them. He enlisted in the RCAF as earlier as September 1940 and served all war through with the RCAF, first in Canada and later over the European Continent. Below right, Percy McLachlan, from British Columbia, was among the few pilots who joined the squadron in March 1944 to reinforce the formerly No.125 Sqn, RCAF with experienced pilots. Sadly, he became one of the first pilots to be killed in action. He had previously served with No.421 (RCAF) Sqn with which he had claimed a confirmed Fw190 in August 1943. (*Author's collection*)

SUMMARY OF THE OPERATIONAL ACTIVITY
No.441 (R.C.A.F.) Squadron

A/C types	First sortie	Last sortie	Total sorties	Tot Sub-type	Lost Ops	Lost Acc	A/C lost	Claims	V-1	Pilot †	PoWs	Eva.
Spitfire V	-	-	-	-	-	1	1	-	-	-	-	-
Spitfire IX	27.03.44	12.05.45	3,169	3,169	21	3	24	49.0	-	11	3	3
Mustang III	-	-	-	-	-	1	1	-	-	1	-	-
Others												
Other causes	-	-	-	-	-	-	-	-	-	-	-	-
Compilation	27.03.44	12.05.45		3,169	21	4	26	49.0	-	12	3	3

MAIN AWARDS

DSO: -

DFC: 8

DFM: -

Points of interest :
- One of the six Canadian Home squadrons to have been sent overseas in 1944.

Unsolved mystery
None.

Statistics :
- Lost one aircraft every 151 sorties.
- 12.50 % of the combat aircraft losses until VE-Day occurred during non operational flights.

BADGE
A silver fox's mask.

The silver fox is an animal indegenous to Canada. It reprensents the squadron's nickname.

MOTTO
STALK AND KILL

Authority: King George VI, December 1945

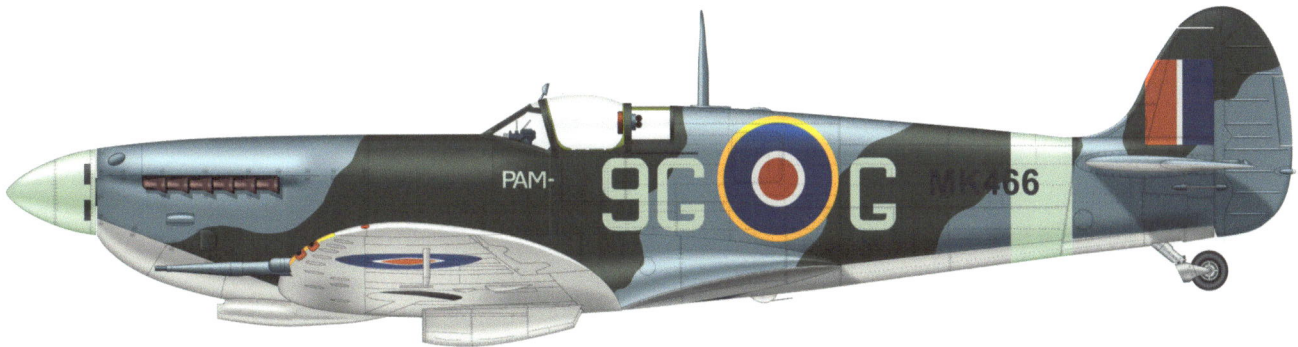

Supermarine Spitfire LF.IXB MK466, Flying Officer Charles A. Graham, Westhampnett, April 1944.
Taken on charge on 20.02.44, MK466 was issued to No.441 Sqn on 13 March and became the mount of Flying Officer Charles A. 'Alex' Graham from Regina, Alberta, Canada. Graham christened his aircraft 'Pam', the name of his wife. He was posted to the squadron in March 1944, one of a few experienced pilots able to share their experience with the newly formed unit, which had evolved from No.125 Sqn, RCAF. Graham had previously served with No.91, 411 (RCAF) and 402 (RCAF) Sqns. His flying career was effectively ended on 12 June 1944, when he crashed on take-off, in this very aircraft, and sustained serious spinal injuries.

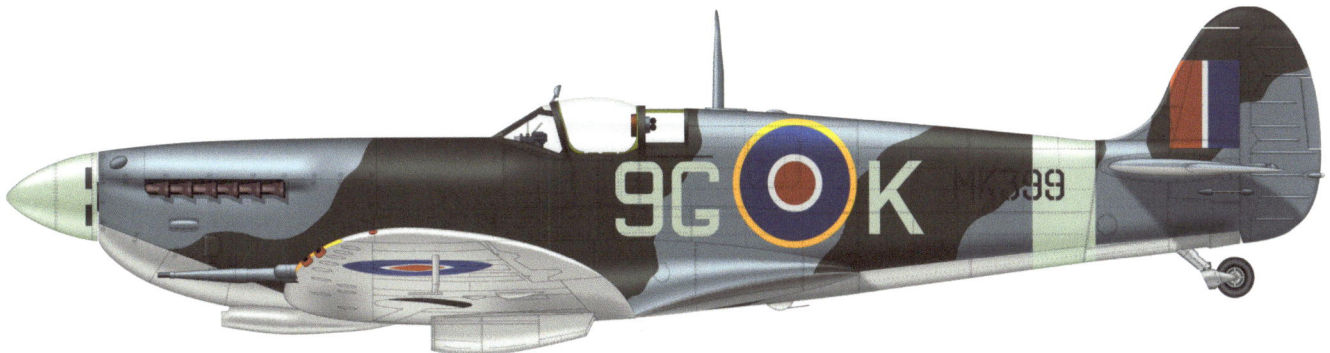

Supermarine Spitfire LF.IXB MK399, Flight Lieutenant Guy E. Mott, Funtington, May 1944.
Taken on charge on 12.02.44, MK466 was issued to No.441 Sqn on 13 March as part of the first batch of Spitfire Mk.IXs. In March and April 1944 it was flown by various pilots until it became the regular mount of the A Flight CO, F/L Guy Mott, by mid-May 1944. However, it was not Mott who was flying MK399 when it was lost after an engine failure on take-off on 15.06.44.

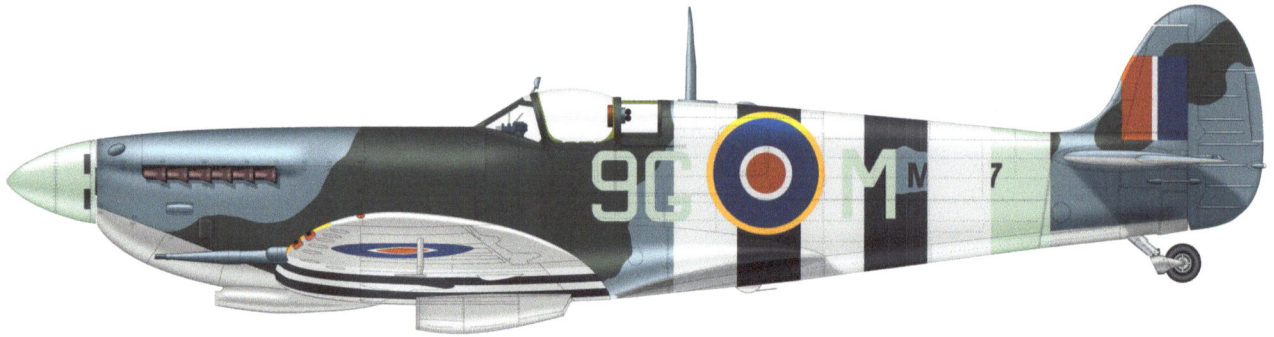

Supermarine Spitfire LF.IXB MK417, Flying Officer Bruce M. MacKenzie, Ford, June 1944.
Taken on charge 09.02.44, MK417 was issued to No.441 Sqn on 12 March, being one of the first Spifire Mk.IXs allocated to the squadron. The machine was assigned to Bruce M. MacKenzie, of Alberta, who had served with No.125 Sqn, RCAF since 1942. He left the squadron in January 1945 when his tour expired. It is noteworthy that during the early part of 441 Sqn's existence many of its pilots used individual letter codes, identical to their surnames, wherever this was possible.

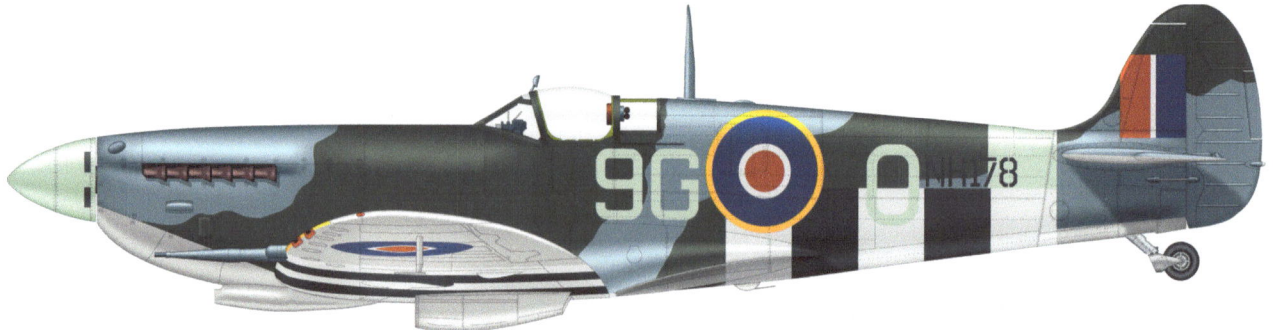

Supermarine Spitfire LF.IXB NH178, Flight Lieutenant William W.L. Brown, B11/Longues (France), August 1944.
The history of this aircraft was rather brief. It was taken on charge by the RAF, 30 April 1944, and stored until issued to No.441 Sqn on 10 August 1944. It was lost, just three days later, when F/L William Brown was shot down by flak, strafing MET during an armed recce NW of Flers. Brown, who had been with the squadron since May, was last seen by his No.2 to go into a spin about 10 m of Vire.
Note that one white stripe has been partially overpainted, with dark green, to highlight the letter 'O'.

Supermarine Spitfire LF.IXB NH209, Flight Lieutenant Guy E. Mott, Hawkinge, October 1944.
The history of this aircraft is only partly known as certain movement details are unrecorded. It was taken on charge on 06.05.44, and the first link with 441 Squadron can be found during October 1944. It is possible it was stored until that time. During the month, this Spitfire became the mount of 'A' Flight Commander's Flight Lieutenant Mott, from Oil Springs, Ontario. He was to become the second of the unit's three aces, and he flew this aircraft until leaving the squadron in December. The aircraft appears to have had an earlier letter code, as the serial is partially overpainted, and the letter 'K' is painted in darker camouflage. NH209 was later passed on to No.1 Sqn in March 1945 as JX-V. Note the red Mapple Leaf painted below the cockpit, a common practice in Canadian squadrons. It was also known as the 'Overseas RCAF roundel'.

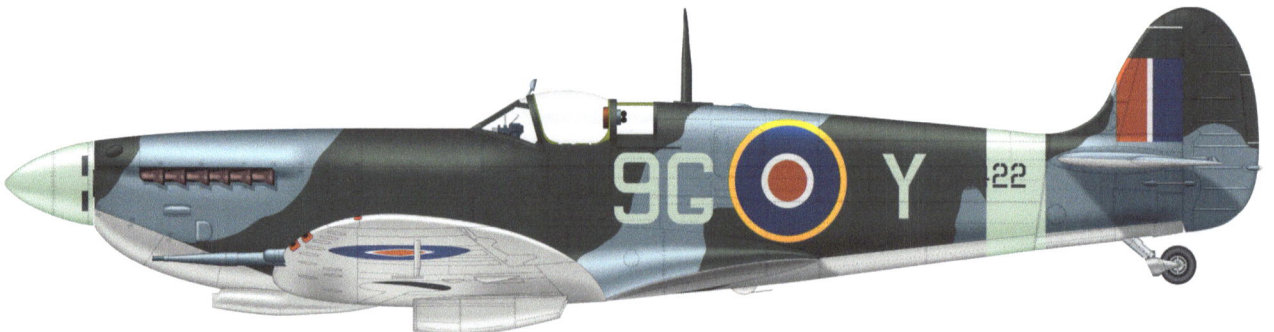

Supermarine Spitfire LF.IXB MA422, Skaebrae, April 1945.
After No.441 Squadron was sent back from France to Skaebrae, in Scotland, it was allocated an assortment of old and new Spitfire Mk.IXs. By February 1945, the Canadians had on strength no less than 29 Spitfire IXs (16 LF.IXs, 12 HF and 1 F), of which MA422 was one. It had been taken on charge 18.07.43 and, during January 1945, was in use with No.303 (Polish) Sqn, being damaged in an accident on 5 March. After repair, somewhere during April, it was allocated to No.441 Sqn, a fact omitted on its movement card. By that time the squadron had returned to normal size, operating a mixture of Spitfires Mk.IXs variants. MA422 was not issued to a specific pilot, and was flown on operations by F/O S. Bregman, WO1 I.J. Hart, F/O J.A. McIntosh, F/L M.E. Monette. After the squadron converted to Mustangs, it was eventually sent to No.80 OTU. Note the serial partially obscured by paint.

North American Mustang Mk.III FZ190, Digby, June 1945.

FZ190 was built as P-51B-5-NA 43-6611 and was stored for about a month before being issued to No.165 Sqn on 312.12.44. It was coded SK-A and like KH495 (see below), it was directly transferred to No.441 Sqn on 31.05.45 when the 165 received Spitfire Mk.IXs. Note this one lacks the fin fillet and also the wing identification band has been overpainted probably with black paint. The D-Day fuselage bands seems to have been also partially overpainted as the area around the letter 'E'.

North American Mustang Mk.III HB876, Digby, June 1945.

Built as P-51C-5-NT 42-103765, it sailed to the UK on S.S. *Chesapeake* and arrived at destination on 25.05.44. It was modified by Lockheed and stored before being issued to No.306 (Polish) Sqn in July 1944 and served later with No.129 Sqn between September and March 1945. It was then sent to No.3501 SU where it is believed all its camouflage paintings was stripped off including the anti-glare panel before to be issued to No.441 Sqn on 14.06.45. Only a small white part located under the nose remains, a part probably taken from another Mustang which still had had the nose identification band. Subsequently it served with No.61 OTU where it was lost in an accident on 27.09.45 and struck off charge.

North American Mustang Mk.III KH466, Digby, June 1945.

No.441 Sqn converted to Mustang IIIs in May 1945, receiving the first aircraft on 31 May 1945, including KH466. Built as P-51C-10-NT 44-10823, it arrived in UK on 10 August 1944. It subsequently served with Nos.118 and 165 Sqns, before reaching No.441 Sqn. When the squadron was disbanded, KH466 was issued to No.315 (Polish) Sqn. This Mustang has the overseas RCAF roundel painted below the cockpit, only a few Mustangs of the squadron are reported to have it painted on. Note the spinner left in Natural Metal Finish instead if white, meaning that the spinner has been recently changed.

North American Mustang Mk.III KH495, Digby, June 1945.

Built as P-51C-10-NT 44-10852, KH495 arrived in the UK on 10.08.44 after having sailed in S.S. *Wolfe*. Modified it was stored at No.20 MU before being issued to No.165 Sqn on 21.12.44 when it became the mount of its last wartime CO, S/L B.E. Gale (RAAF). It was then coded SK-S. When the squadron was re-equipped with Spitfire Mk.IXs after VE-Day, KH495 was transferred direct to No.441 Sqn on 31.05.45 and kept the individual letter 'S' and the squadron codes '9G' were added. The Squadron Leader pennant was still painted on for a while. This Mustang shows many oddities, like the spinner in Natural Metal Finish instead of white, lack of the white nose identification band, and the partial D-Day fuselage bands, which should had been deleted since a long while, are still there. KH495 seems to have flown like this while serving the 165.

AT WAR:
STUDY, HISTORY AND STATISTICS

1922-

The Supermarine
SPITFIRE Mk.V
in the Far East

Vo
Type Desig

Phil H. LISTEMANN

Fighter Leaders
of the RAF, RAAF, RCAF, RNZAF & SAAF in WW2

Volume I

Phil H. Listemann

No.137 Squadron
1941 - 1945

SQUADRONS!

No.2

The Republic
Thunderbolt Mk.I

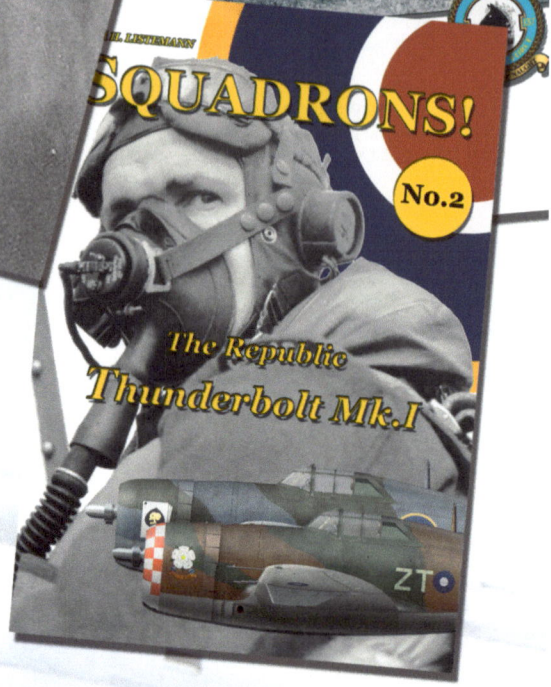

www.RAF-IN-COMBAT.com

- USN Aircraft 1922-1962 -
- Squadrons! -
- RAF, Dominion and Allied squadrons at War -
- Allied Wings -
RAF, DOMINION & ALLIED SQUADRONS
AT WAR: - Famous squadrons of WW2 -
STUDY, HISTORY AND STATISTICS - Fighter Leaders -

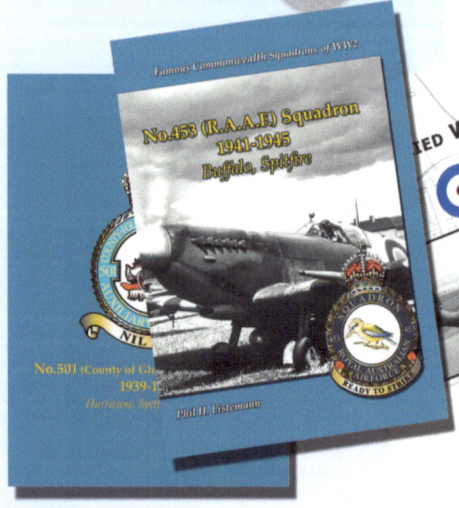

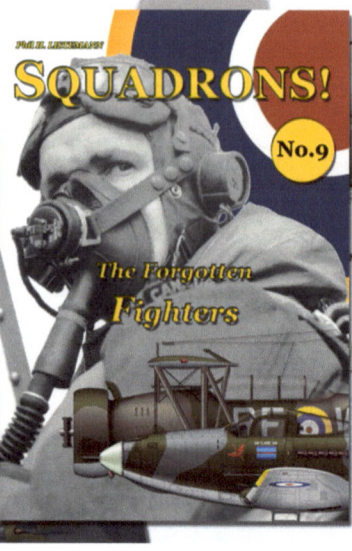

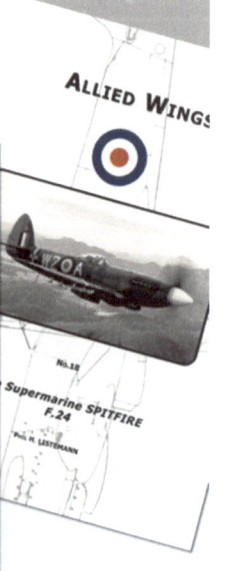

ALLIED WINGS

Famous Commonwealth Squadrons of WW2

No.453 (R.A.A.F.) Squadron
1941-1945
Buffalo, Spitfire

No.131 (County of Kent) Squadron
1941 - 1945

SQUADRONS!

No.9

SQUADRO

The Forgotten
Fighters

Supermarine SPITFIRE
F.24

No.501 (County of Glo
1939-
Hurricane, Spit

Phil H. Listemann

The Handley
Halifax